Sir Francis Drake

by
David Fermer

Alles Digitale zu diesem Buch kann auf der Lernplattform
allango von Ernst Klett Sprachen abgerufen werden. So geht's:

| QR-Code scannen oder **www.allango.net** aufrufen | Buchtitel oder ISBN in der Suche eingeben und auf das Buchcover klicken | Zum Inhalt navigieren, direkt abrufen oder speichern |

Dieses Symbol bedeutet, dass zu einem Buch-Abschnitt
ein digitaler Inhalt verfügbar ist.

Ernst Klett Sprachen
Stuttgart

Digitale Extras:
Zu dieser Geschichte gibt es online (s. die erste Seite des Buches) auch das Hörbuch und einen Wortschatztrainer für alle Vokabeln im Glossar.

1. Auflage   1 ¹⁵ ¹⁴ ¹³ ¹² ¹¹ | 2029 28 27 26 25

Alle Drucke dieser Auflage sind unverändert und können im Unterricht nebeneinander verwendet werden.

Autor: David Fermer
Redaktion: Don Haupt
Layoutkonzeption: Elmar Feuerbach
Umschlaggestaltung: Elmar Feuerbach
Grafik: Matthias Pflügner, Berlin
Tonregie und Schnitt: Andreas Nesic, Stuttgart
Sprecherin: Claire Newcomb
Druck und Bindung: Elanders GmbH, Waiblingen

Printed in Germany
ISBN 978-3-12-572262-0

Contents

Although Sir Francis Drake enjoys legendary status in Britain today, he is a real historical figure. The fleet sent by King Philip II of Spain to invade England in 1588, known as The Spanish Armada, is also fact, not fiction. Here is a short introduction to the most important people involved in this historical event which changed the face of European history:

SIR FRANCIS DRAKE

QUEEN ELIZABETH I

Sir Francis Drake was a famous English seafarer and captain who lived in the 16th century. To the English he was a hero. To the Spanish he was no more than a pirate. He spent years stealing silver and gold from Spanish ships.

Queen Elizabeth I was Queen of England and Ireland from 1558 until her death in 1603. This was a time of economic and cultural growth in England, also known as *The Golden Age*. Elizabeth never married or had any children.

WILLIAM CECIL

FRANCIS WALSINGHAM

William Cecil was the chief advisor of Queen Elizabeth I. He helped the queen make decisions and advised her on policies.

Sir Francis Walsingham was Queen Elizabeth's *spymaster*. He had spies all over Europe to collect information about England's enemies.

PHILIP II

ALONSO DE GUZMÁN

Philip II of Spain was king of Europe's most powerful country from 1556 to 1598. He ruled over one of the world's largest empires, with colonies all over the world.

Alonso de Guzmán was commander-in-chief of the Spanish Armada and the Duke of Medina Sidonia. Unlike Sir Francis Drake, de Guzmán was not a good sea captain.

REVENGE

Revenge was a galleon built in 1577. It was Sir Francis Drake's flagship in the battle of the Spanish Armada. *Revenge* was a relatively small galleon, which made it very fast. It could carry up to 20 heavy cannons. The ship was captured by the Spanish in 1591 and sunk.

The sun is going down over the dark waters of the Atlantic. From the deck of his ship, Sir Francis Drake looks at the green shores of Spain in the distance. In the port of Cádiz people are lighting candles in their homes, getting ready for the night.

"We wait for darkness," Drake tells his second-in-command, William Burrows. Flags are waved from the deck of Drake's galleon, sending signals to the other ships. Red, blue and white flags. Four galleons and twenty other ships, smaller in size, are waiting on the water.

Darkness falls. The ships put up their sails. The wind is perfect. Slowly the English fleet sails into the enemy's harbour.

"Wait for my command before firing," Drake tells his officers.

On the gun deck, the sailors have their cannons ready.

Drake brings his fleet into the harbour. When he sees the Spanish boats, he gives the command to turn his galleon so that the cannons can be fired from the side.

The Spanish see the English ships. Drake can hear the Spanish sailors shouting in Spanish. Alarm bells ring. But it is too late. Drake's magnificent galleon has already turned. Its cannons are aimed at the Spanish ships.

"Fire!" Drake commands.

A huge explosion rings out of the galleon's belly. Smoke rises into the night air. The cannon balls fly into the Spanish ships. Masts fall. Men scream. Shouting. Chaos.

"Fire!" Drake calls again, and again, and again. The Spanish hardly have time to load their cannons.

"We will teach these Spanish Catholics a lesson!" Drake tells his officers. "No Spaniard will ever invade England. Not with these ships!"

Fighting goes on all night and the next day. Some English ships drop anchor in the port. English soldiers go into the city, killing and plundering.

Drake destroys one Spanish ship after another. His officers count more than thirty boats.

Drake knows that his queen will be pleased with him.

"These godless Protestants! Who do they think they are?"

Philip II, the King of Spain, is not a happy man. Nor is Alonso de Guzmán, the commander of the Spanish navy.

"We have been building this fleet for years!" shouts Philip, hitting the table with his hand. His glass of wine falls over, spilling onto his papers. "Years of work for nothing! Millions of *reales* for nothing!"

Alonso de Guzmán looks at his feet. There is nothing for him to say. Philip is right: it is a disaster. A terrible disaster.

"Who is this Francis Drake?" Philip asks.

Alonso de Guzmán raises his head and looks at his king for the first time. "He is a pirate!" says the Spanish commander, hissing like a snake. "A thief!"

"A pirate maybe, but he is a good seaman!" King Philip replies.

"For years Drake has been attacking our ships in the Caribbean, stealing our gold and destroying our ships. He even attacked the port of San Augustín in Florida."

De Guzmán points at a map of the world. The islands of the Caribbean, the finger-like peninsula of Florida, all in Spanish hands.

"Queen Elizabeth of England says she has nothing to do with him," de Guzmán continues. "She says he works alone. But the queen doesn't speak the truth. Elizabeth knows Drake. She knows him well. She helps him in secret. She was the one who sent him to Cádiz, I am sure of it."

"If what you say is true, then we must strike back," King Philip says. "We will invade England and overthrow Queen Elizabeth."

Alonso de Guzmán bows before his king. "Your words are my command."

King Philip takes a bag of gold from his table.

"You have one year, de Guzmán. One year to rebuild the Spanish fleet." He gives the bag of gold to de Guzmán. "You will have money, lots of money, and men and supplies. Everything you need. Next year the Spanish fleet will sail to England and put an end to the Protestant witch - once and for all. The new fleet will be the best in the world. So strong, so fast, so powerful, that nothing can stop it. This fleet I will call the *Armada*."

“Your Majesty, we bring good news!”

William Cecil, the queen's advisor, comes into the chamber where the queen is getting dressed. Two servant women are putting on her wig and powdering her face with white make-up.

“Good morning, Cecil!” says the queen. “Please, sit down.”

William Cecil is an old man with a long white beard. He has known the queen almost all his life. He walks with a stick and is happy to sit down.

A younger man, Francis Walsingham, follows him into the room. His beard has only a few grey hairs. His eyes are small and black, like a bird's. He stands in the corner of the room and listens to Cecil.

“Drake destroyed thirty-seven Spanish ships in Cádiz harbour, Your Majesty!” Cecil reports. “The Spanish will never be able to attack us now.”

“I do not agree with you,” says Walsingham. “The Spanish are rich. They have gold from the Americas. And they hate us. They know that if they do not stop us, they will lose their colonies in the Netherlands.”

“The Netherlands are not important!” says Cecil.

"The Netherlands are Protestant," says Walsingham. "Like us."

The queen stands up and smiles at Walsingham, the man she calls her 'spymaster'. Her teeth are black. Too much sugar in the royal court.

"Do not fight, gentlemen." She looks out of the window. On the horizon she can see the Tower of London. "What do you think we should do, Cecil?"

"Send Drake back to the Caribbean," says Cecil. "Tell him to take all the gold he can from the Spanish. That will stop them from rebuilding the fleet."

"And you, Walsingham?" the queen asks.

"Bring Drake back to England. Make our fleet strong. Prepare for the Spanish invasion, for it will come."

The queen nods. A flock of black birds flies past the window. They land on the green grass below. The queen's dog runs up to them and chases them away, barking and showing his teeth.

"I have already told Drake to come home," Elizabeth says. "Nobody knows the Spanish better than him. He has singed the beard of the King of Spain. If Philip attacks us, I will tell Drake to burn more than just his beard!"

The streets of London are full of people. They wave English flags and call out Sir Francis Drake's name. "Drake, Drake, Drake!"

Some of them even call out his Spanish nickname, laughing at the Spanish and their king. "*El Draque! El Draque! El Draque!*" The dragon.

Drake rides through the streets of London on his white horse. William Burrows and his chief officers are with him. The queen has asked to speak to him. Sir Francis thinks he knows why. No one hates the Spanish Catholics more than he does.

Drake comes from a Protestant family. His father was a farmer. As a boy the Catholics forced the family to leave their farm because of their religion. Drake was nine years old at the time. After they were forced to leave, he and his twelve brothers and sisters lived on an old boat on a river. It was there, on that boat, that Drake found his love of the sea.

The queen is waiting for Drake in her palace at Hampton Court. Every few weeks she moves to another palace so that the rooms can be aired and cleaned and the toilets emptied.

"You have done well, sir," the queen tells Drake when he comes into her chamber. "But we are not safe from the Spanish yet."

"I know, Your Majesty. They are rebuilding the fleet."

"They will not let Cádiz happen again," Elizabeth says. "We will have to wait for them to come to us. And when they do, I want you to be ready for them."

Drake bows. "I will do whatever you want, Your Majesty."

"You will be Vice Admiral," the queen tells him. "Second-in-command."

Drake looks at the queen in horror. "But ... who is the commander?"

"Lord Howard of Effingham."

"Lord Howard?" cries Drake. He hates Lord Howard. Howard is the queen's cousin. "But why, Your Majesty? I am a better seaman."

"I know," the queen says. "But Lord Howard is High Admiral. He is the face of the English navy. And you are the heart. Can I trust you, Drake? Will you do your job? Will you stop the Spanish Armada?"

Drake kneels before his queen and kisses her hand. "I will, Majesty, I will."

The port of Plymouth, on the south coast of England, is buzzing with activity. Hundreds of men are building new ships for the English fleet. Every day dozens of trees are transported into the city from the nearby forests. Carpenters cut the trees and make ships from the wood.

In the harbour women sit in groups making sails while others cook for the seamen and carpenters. Cannons are cleaned, gunpowder is carried onto the ships, men wash the decks with water.

Every day a new ship arrives. The queen is not just building ships, she is buying them too. The new fleet has to be big - the biggest fleet England has ever had. Sir Francis Drake stands in the harbour with his commander, Lord Howard of Effingham, watching the people working.

"We need more cannons," says Lord Howard, looking at his galleon, the Ark Royal. "I will write to the queen and ask her for more money."

"No, my Lord," Drake says. "Cannons are heavy. They slow us down. We must be fast and flexible to beat the Spanish."

Lord Howard laughs. "You are wrong, sir. It is cannons which win wars. Speed is not important. War is not a race."

"It will be with the Spanish," Drake says. "When they come, they will come quickly. If we are too slow, they will be in London before us."

"Nonsense!" cries Lord Howard, laughing. "You have spent too much time in the Caribbean. Cannons are what we need. Lots of them!"

Lord Howard walks off. He goes along the gangplank onto the Ark Royal.

"Problems?" asks William, who overheard the discussion.

"Lord Howard is a politician not a seaman," Drake says. "If we do what he says, we will lose. I do not want to live in a Catholic England. Ever."

Drake and William watch Lord Howard go over the deck and disappear into his cabin.

"You must help me to stop him," says Drake. "Together you and I must take the command of the English fleet. Only we can beat the Spanish Armada. If we leave things to Howard, then it will end in disaster."

On a patch of green grass in Plymouth, a group of four men are playing bowls. Bowls is a game where one player throws a small red ball called a 'jack' onto the grass and the others take turns to roll their bigger balls – the bowls – as close to the jack as possible. William wins the round.

"The last round decides the winner," he says, picking up the red jack to start the next round.

"And I will win it!" says his friend and commander, Sir Francis Drake.

William smiles and throws the jack onto the grass. Francis steps up to the line and rolls his bowl onto the grass. His bowl touches the jack. To beat him, William will have to knock away his bowl.

"Sir! Sir!" An officer comes running up the hill to the lawn. "Sir Francis! We have been looking for you everywhere!"

The officer is out of breath.

"What is it, Hawkins?" Drake asks.

"The Spanish …" gasps Hawkins. "The Armada … is coming!"

Drake looks down the coast. On the horizon a fire is burning. Another fire is burning on the next cliff. And the next and the next. The signal.

Francis turns back to his game of bowls. "Before we do anything, we must finish the game."

William looks at Francis in surprise. "But Francis, the Spanish will be here by nightfall!"

"Exactly," says Francis. "And by then we will be gone. The English fleet must leave Plymouth before the Armada enters the harbour, or else they will do to us what we did to them in Cádiz."

"Let us leave now!" says William.

"First we finish the game," says Drake. "It's your turn, William."

"But Francis!"

Francis holds up his hand. "Look at the sea, William! We cannot leave now. Don't you see? The tide is out. We have to wait for high tide. Then we will set sail. Hawkins, go back to the harbour and tell Lord Howard we will be leaving in one hour. And now, William, please, play the game!"

"Lights out!" The order is passed from ship to ship. The officers speak in whispers. "Lights out! Lights out!"

It is night. There is not a star in the sky. A grey fog hangs in the air as the English fleet sails out of Plymouth harbour. The English ships put out their lights. Drake can hardly see the ship next to his.

Out at sea, on the horizon, Drake can see the lights of the Spanish Armada. They are coming closer. Drake counts more than twenty galleons and at least a hundred smaller ships. He knows they have many more cannons than the English fleet.

"Go west along the coast," says Drake as the English fleet sails onto the open sea.

"West?" asks William, surprised. "But that's the wrong direction, sir! If we go west, the Armada will be in front of us!"

"That is not a problem," Drake replies. "We are faster than they are. We can catch up with them tomorrow and attack them from behind. Now we have to move quickly. If they trap us here in the harbour, they will destroy us."

William gives the command. Drake's galleon, Revenge, leads the English fleet out of Plymouth harbour. They disappear into the night. Not a single cannon is shot. Only the sound of the waves can be heard.

The next morning Drake gets a message from Lord Howard. He wants to see his Vice Admiral. Drake's officers lower a rowing boat onto the water and row their commander over to the Ark Royal.

On the Ark Royal, Lord Howard is having breakfast in the captain's cabin. Red wine and chicken, hot potatoes, fresh vegetables. A feast for a king.

"My Lord," says Drake as he comes into the room. "You called for me?"

Lord Howard finishes eating and stands up. For a moment Drake thinks Howard is going to shout at him, but he doesn't. Instead he holds out his hand. "I wanted to say thank you, Sir Francis. Thank you for saving the English fleet last night. From now on I will listen to what you have to say."

"My pleasure, my Lord," says Drake, shaking Howard's hand. "If you and I work together, then we can defeat the Spanish Armada."

"Tell me, what should we do?"

Lord Howard's servants have cleared away the breakfast. Drake and his officers are standing around Howard's table. A map of the British Isles is spread out on the table. The English Channel. The North Sea. Scotland and Ireland. At the bottom of the map: France and the Netherlands. Francis puts his finger on a town in northern France.

"Our spies tell us there are 30,000 Spanish soldiers waiting here at Gravelines," Drake says. "Before attacking England, the Armada will stop at the French coast to pick them up."

"How long does the Armada need to get there?" asks Lord Howard.

"Six days. Maybe a week."

"We must stop them before they pick up the soldiers," Howard says.

Drake agrees. They decide to attack the Armada. They will divide their fleet into two groups and attack the Spanish from both sides.

With the plan now made, Drake and his officers row back to the Revenge.

As Drake goes to his cabin, he sees a small boy on deck. The boy looks no older than ten.

"What are you doing on this ship?" Drake asks. "You are a boy!"

"Yes, but one day I will be a great seaman like you!" the boy answers.

"Maybe you will ..." Drake says, looking at the boy from head to toe. His face is dirty; his hair looks like a bird's nest; his clothes are full of holes. "But first you must go to school and learn to read and write."

"School is for girls!" the boy says. "Reading is for priests."

"There is your first mistake, boy," says Drake, holding up his finger. "I have learned as much from books as I have by travelling around the world on this ship. A life of one without the other is an empty life. You must go to school if you want to captain a galleon like this one."

"If you say so, sir," says the boy.

"I do. And when we get back to England, I will see to it personally that you go back to school. This galleon is no place for children. Now go below deck and read a book!"

After days at sea, the wind changes. The Spanish Armada cannot continue towards France. The Spanish commander, the Duke of Medina, can see the English fleet coming from behind.

The English fleet has divided into two and is coming at the Spanish from both sides. The Duke of Medina sees the danger. He doesn't want to be attacked. Not now. The Armada must continue, even if they have to sail in the wrong direction.

The duke tells his officers to form a half-moon. This formation is the best defence against the English.

On the Revenge, Drake watches the Spanish Armada regroup. He knows it is too dangerous to attack them now. He tells his officers to fire some cannons anyway. The English cannons can fire further than the Spanish.

The sailors on the gun deck think this is a bad idea. The Spanish are too far away. They fire their cannons, as Drake commanded, but the cannonballs land in the water.

"Keep firing!" Drake orders.

"But why?" asks William. "We are too far away."

"We must make the Spanish break their formation," Drake says. "If the wind doesn't change, they will have to stop at the Isle of Wight. Then we can attack them."

But later in the day the wind does change. The Spanish can turn around and sail towards France. The Duke of Medina is happy.

"The Spanish have left behind two ships," Drake's officer tells him. "We hit them with our cannons. The ships are damaged."

Drake smiles. He was once a pirate. He has never lost his love of gold.

"Let us go back and see what is on the ships," Drake says.

"But if we plunder the ships, we will lose contact with the English fleet."

"We can catch up with them later," Drake says. "There is gold on those ships. And gunpowder! We need both."

As night falls, Drake puts out all the lights on the Revenge and leaves the English fleet. He sails back to the two Spanish ships and sends his men on board to take the gold. "Once a pirate, always a pirate!" thinks William.

" Where were you last night?" asks Lord Howard at breakfast the next day. He has called Drake to his ship again.

"We got lost," Drake says, but it's not true. He was plundering the Spanish ships.

Lord Howard is angry. The English fleet had to wait for the Revenge to catch up with them.

"The Armada has stopped," Lord Howard tells him. "They are waiting off the French coast near Gravelines, just as you said. But the ships are so close together, we cannot attack them."

"Are they still in a half-moon formation?" Drake asks.

Lord Howard nods. "If we attack them, they will destroy us."

"We must break the formation," Drake says.

"How?"

Drake looks out of the window. He sees two smaller ships next to the Ark Royal. The ships are old and in need of repair. Drake has an idea.

"We can make hellburners!" Drake says.

"Hellburners?" asks Lord Howard. "What are they?"

"Fireships! We take ten or twelve ships, old ones, and set them on fire. Then we send them into the Spanish fleet! That will break the formation and then we can attack them."

"Twelve ships?" Lord Howard doesn't look too happy about the idea. "We cannot lose twelve ships!"

"Even if they win the war for us?" Drake asks.

Lord Howard looks out of the window at the old ships. In the end, he agrees. "But only eight ships, Drake. Only eight!"

That night Drake's men pack eight ships full of gunpowder and wood. They set the ships on fire and send them into the Spanish Armada.

Drake and Howard watch the burning fireships float towards the Armada. The Spanish panic. They raise their sails and break their formation.

"Now we attack!" says Drake. "Will you give the command, my Lord?"

"Aye, aye sir!" says Howard. "With pleasure!"

"Sir Francis! Sir Francis! The Spanish are going north!"

Francis Drake is asleep in his cabin.

"Wake up, Sir Francis! Come and see!"

Drake slowly gets out of bed. His head hurts from drinking too much red wine. He opens his cabin door. The 10-year-old boy is standing outside.

"You?!"

"We have passed the Thames Estuary!" the boy says. "The Spanish are going north."

Drake smiles. "Then London is safe!" he says.

"The whole of England is safe!" the boy cries. "The Spanish will never invade us now! They're finished!"

Drake quickly gets dressed and follows the boy onto the deck. The Spanish Armada is spread out all over the North Sea. The English are attacking the slowest Spanish ships. The Armada is falling apart.

"You are right, my boy," Drake says. "They are going north. And we will not let them come back!"

"The Spanish will have to sail around Scotland and Ireland and into the North Atlantic," says William when Drake joins him on deck.

Drake smiles. "The sea will finish what we have started. The North Atlantic is more dangerous than we are! The Armada will never return to Spain in one piece."

Lord Howard comes onto the Revenge to celebrate their victory.

"How long will we chase them?" Drake asks Lord Howard.

"We will follow them to Scotland and leave them when they have no other option than to go into the North Atlantic," Lord Howard answers.

"And then?"

"Then we will return to London."

Drake nods in agreement. He looks down at the small boy standing next to him. "And when we are back in London, you, my boy, will go to school!"

"But Sir Francis ...!" cries the boy.

Francis raises his finger to silence the boy. "Now, now! You cannot argue with a Vice Admiral! An order is an order!"

"Your Majesty! Sir Francis Drake is here!"

The queen is playing bowls on the grass at Windsor Castle. It is a warm summer day. The sun is shining. The birds are singing in the trees.

Drake rides his horse through the gates of Windsor Castle where the queen likes to spend her summers. He jumps off his horse and walks across the grass towards the queen.

"Welcome, Sir Francis, you are just in time for a game," Elizabeth says.

"I fear I am out of practice," Drake answers. "I have been at sea for four weeks. You will win easily, Your Majesty."

"That is good for me," says the queen. "I like to win."

"But I do not like to lose," Drake says with a smile.

"So I hear. That is good. The battle against the Spanish is won, but the war is not over, Drake. You would do anything for your queen, am I right?"

Drake nods.

"The Duke of Medina has returned to Spain," the queen tells him, picking up the red jack. "The Armada lost almost half of its ships. Walsingham thinks that

more than 20,000 Spanish sailors died. You worked well with Lord Howard, but now I want you to go back to your old ways."

"My old ways?"

"The Spanish still call you a pirate, Sir Francis. A 'dragon'. Your queen would be happy if you went back to that old tradition."

"You want me to go back to the Caribbean as a pirate?"

The queen nods. "Unofficially, of course. See what you can do out there. Take their gold, take their ports, take whatever you can. Anything that hurts the Spanish is good for England."

"Very well," Drake agrees. "Your wish is my command."

The queen throws the jack onto the grass. Drake picks up his bowl. He is about to roll it onto the grass when he stops. "And ... what if I beat you at this game, Your Majesty?" he asks.

"Then I will send you to the Tower of London!"

Drake laughs and rolls his bowl onto the grass. "I see. Then I have no choice, Your Majesty. I wish you the best of luck!"

THE END

Historical background

 The Spanish Armada took place at a time of great change in European history. For centuries, Europe had been Catholic, but with the Protestant Reformation, which started in Germany in the early 16th century, Europe became religiously divided. Protestantism soon began to spread to countries like the Netherlands, Scandinavian countries and Britain. The king at the time, Henry VIII, was a devout Catholic, but he had a problem: he wanted to leave his first wife, Catherine of Aragon, and marry again. For Henry, it was very important to have a son who could inherit his throne after his death, but with Catherine, he only had a daughter. When Henry asked for the Pope's permission to divorce Catherine, the Pope refused, and so Henry broke away from the Catholic Church and created his own church, which he called the *Church of England*. This was not really a Protestant church, but for the Pope and his allies, especially the King of Spain, the Church of England was the enemy.

When Henry VIII died, he left his throne to his only son, Edward, who was crowned King of England at the age of 9. Edward's reign was very short, because he died from an illness at the age of only 15. Henry VIII's first daughter, Mary, the only daughter of Catherine of Aragon, then became Queen of England. Like her mother, Mary was a devout Catholic. King Philip I of Spain saw an opportunity to create a powerful Catholic alliance and quickly arranged for his son, the future Philip II of Spain, to marry Mary in 1554. If Mary and Philip had ever had a son, the history of Europe might have been very different. But they didn't have any children. Mary, who was 37 when she married Philip and 11 years older than her husband, died only four years later. Her half-sister, Elizabeth, the daughter of Henry VIII's second wife, then took the throne as Queen Elizabeth I. Unlike Mary, Elizabeth was not a Catholic. As England grew politically and economically during her reign, and alliances were formed with Protestants in the Netherlands, England became more and more of a problem for Philip II of Spain. When privateers like Sir Francis Drake began to attack and loot Spanish ships bringing gold from the South American colonies, Philip II decided it was time to stop the *Protestant Queen* once and for all. He built the Spanish Armada in the hope of defeating the English and becoming King of England once again.

The life of Sir Francis Drake

Francis Drake was born around 1540, as the eldest of twelve children. Most of the people in his home county of Devon were Catholic, but Drake's family was Protestant. The Drakes suffered under religious persecution and left their home when Drake was 9. In their new home, on the coast of Kent, Drake's father became a vicar in the *Church of England* and began working for the Royal Navy. This was Drake's first contact with sailors and the sea.

Drake made his first big expedition to sea when he was just 23 years old. His cousin, John Hawkins, owned a small fleet of ships, and the two young men set sail to Africa, where they captured slaves to be sold in the New World (America). When their fleet was attacked by the Spanish on the Mexican coast, only Drake and Hawkins managed to escape. This experience, together with his experiences as a child, made him hate Catholics, in particular the Spanish. Drake began to work independently as a privateer. He started attacking the Spanish ships which were transporting silver and gold from South America to Madrid. Such expeditions often lasted more than a year.

When Queen Elizabeth I heard of Drake's success, she sent him on a secret mission to attack the Spanish. He left England with a total of five ships, including his own: *The Pelican*. After many storms and sea battles, all the ships were destroyed, apart from *The Pelican*. Still Drake sailed on, renaming his ship *The Golden Hind*, and he became the first English captain to sail around the world. A replica of The *Golden Hind* can still be seen in London today.

Only a year after the Spanish Armada, Drake was back at sea again, fighting for the queen. He attacked Spanish ships, but he was beginning to lose his touch. In the expedition of 1589, he lost 12,000 lives and 20 ships. A few years later, Drake set sail once again with his cousin, Hawkins, to loot gold from the Spanish. It was to be his last expedition. Drake was in his mid-50s, quite old by Elizabethan standards, and while attacking the Spanish off Panama, he died of dysentery.

Drake died a hero to the English people and a villain to the Spanish. Today, there is much debate about whether Drake was a good or bad man, but there is little doubt that he was a brilliant sailor.

Exercises

Episode 1

Choose the correct answer.

On the gun deck…
A) ☐ the sailors have a party.
B) ☐ the sailors have their cannons ready.
C) ☐ the sailors are lighting candles.

The English attack with…
A) ☐ 4 galleons and 20 smaller ships.
B) ☐ 4 galleons and 21 smaller ships.
C) ☐ 5 galleons and 22 smaller ships.

Drake's fleet is near…
A) ☐ the Caribbean Islands.
B) ☐ the harbour of Cádiz.
C) ☐ the green shores of England.

Drake thinks that…
A) ☐ the king will be pleased with him.
B) ☐ the Spanish are Protestants.
C) ☐ the Spanish will never invade England.

Episode 2

There is a mistake in each of the following sentences. Find the wrong keywords and write down the correct words.

1. De Guzmán is the commander of the Spanish army. _____

2. It has taken years to build the Spanish castles. _____

3. De Guzmán thinks that Drake is a prince. _____

4. King Philip thinks that Drake is a good cook. _____

5. De Guzmán has one year to sink the Spanish fleet. _____

6. Alonso will have enough money, men and spies. _____

Episode 3

In episode 3 the queen and her advisors discuss whether Drake should go to the Caribbean or come back to England. What reasons do they give?

Go to the Caribbean	Come back to England

What do you think Drake should do?

_____

_____

Episode 4

Read the summary and find the mistakes. Correct the text and copy it into your exercise book.

When Drake arrives in Plymouth, people are waving Spanish flags to welcome him. They call out his Spanish nickname *El Draque*! The monkey.
Drake comes from a Catholic family. Drake's father was a sailor. When the Protestants forced his family to leave their house in London, he lived on an old farm.
Drake is on his way to the king on his black donkey. The king is very pleased with him. Drake says that they are not yet safe. He thinks that the French are rebuilding their harbour. The king wants to be ready when the Spanish attack. He makes Drake the commander of the English fleet. His second-in-command will be Lord Howard – the king's brother. Drake loves Lord Howard. Lord Howard is also a better seaman than Drake is.
Drake will do what the king wants of him. He will help the Spanish Armada.

Episode 5

Collect important keywords for episode 5 and write them in your exercise book. Try to retell the episode using your notes. Work with your neighbour and practise.

Episode 6

Put the questions into the right order and answer them in complete sentences! Check with your partner.

1. playing – Drake – are – game – and – what – William?
2. you – game – play – how – the – do?
3. for – looking – Hawkins – Drake – is – why?
4. the – to – the – of – how – Spanish – news – react – Drake – does – Armada?
5. enter – the – will – harbour – when – Spanish – Armada – the?
6. the – Plymouth – why – English – leave – fleet – can't?

Episode 7

Read episodes 5 – 7 again and have a look at the following speech bubbles. Copy the speech bubbles into your exercise book and for each one write who says this and in which situation.

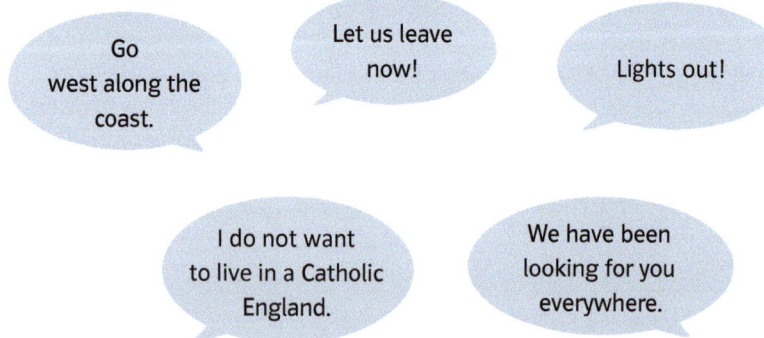

Episode 8

Complete the map (hint: 4-8 countries, 9-11 cities).

1. _____
2. _____
3. _____
4. _____
5. _____
6. _____
7. _____
8. _____
9. _____
10. _____
11. _____

After reading episode 11, can you draw the course of the Spanish Armada on the map?

Exercises

Episode 9

What happens first? Put these sentences into the correct order.

☐ They fire their cannons, but the cannonballs land in the water.

☐ At nightfall, the Revenge leaves the English fleet.

☐ The Spanish manage to get away but leave two ships behind.

☐ The Spanish commander can see the English fleet coming from behind.

☐ Drake tells his officers to fire some cannons.

☐ Drake decides to see what is on the ships.

☐ The duke tells his officers to form a half-moon.

☐ Later in the day, the wind changes.

☐ Drake sends his men on board to look for gold and gunpowder.

Episode 10

Crossword – **across:** 5. .... Howard   6. to steal gold (from a ship)
7. aggressive move, go on the offensive   9. half-moon .... 10. to mend sth
11. *zerstören* (engl.) – **down:** 1. to not sink   2. a creative new thought
3. hellburners   4. explosive mixture   8. an order

Episode 11

Match the sentence halves.

His head hurts	a Vice Admiral.
The Spanish will never	celebrate their victory.
Drake quickly gets dressed and	follows the boy onto the deck.
The Spanish Armada is spread	from drinking too much red wine.
The Spanish will have to	invade us now.
Lord Howard comes onto the Revenge to	leave them when they have to go into the North Atlantic.
We will follow them to Scotland and	out all over the North Sea.
He looks down at the small boy	sail around Scotland and Ireland.
You cannot argue with	standing next to him.

Episode 12

1. True or false? Circle the answer!
   a) The Armada lost almost all of its ships.   T / F
   b) The queen wants Drake to go back to the Caribbean as a pirate.   T / F

2. Fill in the gaps with the correct prepositions.
   Drake rides his horse _____ the gates of Windsor Castle. He jumps _____ his horse and walks _____ the grass _____ the queen. The battle _____ the Spanish is won. Drake would do anything _____ his queen.

3. Answer the questions in complete sentences.
   a) What is the queen doing when Drake arrives?
   b) Why doesn't Drake want to play with her?
   c) What are Drake's 'old ways'?
   d) What will the queen do with Drake if she loses the game?

The characters

figure Persönlichkeit
fleet [fliːt] Flotte
to invade [ɪnˈveɪd] einmarschieren
introduction Vorstellung, Einführung
involved beteiligt
seafarer Seefahrer
economic wirtschaftlich
growth Wachstum
chief advisor Hauptberater
policy Politik
spy [spaɪ] Spion
to rule herrschen
commander-in-chief Oberbefehls-
   haber
galleon [ˈɡælɪən] Galeone
to capture [ˈkæptʃə] einfangen,
   hier: kapern

Episode 1

to light *hier:* anzünden
second-in-command stellvertreten-
   der Kommandeur
to wave *hier:* schwenken
Darkness falls. Die Dunkelheit
   bricht herein.
to put up a sail ein Segel hissen
command Befehl
to fire *hier:* abfeuern
officer Offizier
sailor Matrose, Seemann
alarm bell Alarmglocke
magnificent großartig
to aim zielen
to ring out ertönen
belly Bauch

to rise [raɪz] *hier:* aufsteigen
mast Schiffsmast
hardly kaum
to load laden
to drop anchor [ˈæŋkə] Anker werfen
port Hafen
to plunder [ˈplʌndə] plündern
to destroy zerstören
to be pleased with sb mit jdm zu-
   frieden sein

Episode 2

nor und auch nicht
navy Marine
to spill verschütten
real [reɪˈɑːl] *spanische Währung im
   16. Jh.*
disaster Katastrophe
to raise [reɪz] heben, anheben
to hiss zischen
to attack angreifen
peninsula Halbinsel
truth Wahrheit
to strike back zurückschlagen
to overthrow sb jdn stürzen
to bow [baʊ] sich verbeugen
to rebuild wieder aufbauen
supplies Nachschub, Material
once and for all endgültig

Episode 3

Your Majesty [ˈmædʒəsti] Eure
   Majestät
chamber Schlafgemach
wig Perücke
to powder pudern

the Americas Nord-, Süd- und
  Mittelamerika
the Netherlands die Niederlande
royal court Königshof
horizon [həˈraɪzn] Horizont
for *hier:* denn
a flock of birds Vogelschwarm
to singe [sɪndʒ] ansengen, ver-
sengen

Episode 4

dragon Drache
to force sb jdn zwingen
at the time damals
to air lüften
vice admiral Vizeadmiral
to trust vertrauen
to kneel before sb vor jdm nieder-
knien

Episode 5

is buzzing with activity es herrscht
  reger Betrieb
dozen [ˈdʌzn] Dutzend
carpenter Zimmermann
gunpowder Schießpulver
to slow sb down jdn verlangsamen
flexible *hier:* wendig, beweglich
to beat *hier:* besiegen
speed Geschwindigkeit
Nonsense! Unsinn!
Caribbean [kærɪˈbiːən] Karibik
gangplank [ˈgæŋplæŋk] Landungssteg
to overhear zufällig mithören
politician [pɒlɪˈtɪʃn] Politiker
cabin Kabine
to leave sth to sb jdm etwas über-
  lassen

Episode 6

patch Flecken
to touch berühren
to knock away *hier:* wegstoßen
lawn [lɔːn] Rasen
to be out of breath [breθ] außer
  Atem sein
cliff Klippe
nightfall Einbruch der Nacht
the tide is out es ist Ebbe
to set sail Segel setzen

Episode 7

order Befehl
to be passed (on) *hier:* weitergege-
  ben werden
to speak in whispers flüstern
along entlang
direction Richtung
to catch up einholen
to trap (in einer Falle) fangen
to lead anführen
feast [fiːst] Festessen
instead stattdessen
My pleasure! Gern geschehen!

Episode 8

to divide [dɪˈvaɪd] teilen
to captain befehligen
below (nach) unten

Episode 9

to continue *hier:* weitersegeln
towards in Richtung (darauf zu)
to form a half-moon einen Halb-
  mond bilden
defence Verteidigung

to regroup sich neu formieren
further ['fɜːðə] weiter
damaged beschädigt
contact Kontakt

Episode 10

in need of repair reparatur-
bedürftig
to set on fire in Brand setzen
to float treiben, schwimmen
to panic in Panik geraten
pleasure Vergnügen

Episode 11

wine Wein
estuary ['estjʊəri] Flussmündung
finished *hier:* erledigt
to be spread out *hier:* verteilt
to fall apart auseinanderbrechen
to sail around umsegeln
to join sb sich zu jdm gesellen
to return zurückkehren
victory Sieg
option ['ɒpʃn] Wahl
agreement Zustimmung
to silence sb jdn zum Schweigen
bringen
to argue ['ɑːgjuː] argumentieren

Episode 12

to fear *hier:* befürchten
to be out of practice aus der Übung
sein
to go back to one's old ways wieder
in seine alten Gewohnheiten fallen
choice Wahl

Additional information

to take place stattfinden
divided *hier:* uneinig
to spread sich verbreiten
devout [dɪ'vaʊt] fromm
to inherit erben
permission Erlaubnis
to refuse ablehnen
to break away *hier:* sich lossagen,
abkehren
ally ['ælaɪ] Verbündeter
to crown krönen
opportunity Gelegenheit
alliance [ə'laɪəns] Bündnis
to arrange sth etwas arrangieren
privateer [praɪvə'tɪə] Freibeuter
to loot plündern

county Grafschaft
to suffer leiden
persecution [pɜːsɪ'kjuːʃn] Verfolgung
vicar ['vɪkə] Pfarrer
expedition Reise, Expedition
slave Sklave
to escape entkommen
experience Erfahrung
to transport transportieren
to last (an)dauern
a total of insgesamt
including einschließlich
apart from abgesehen von
replica Nachbau
dysentery ['dɪsəntri] *entzündliche
Erkrankung des Dickdarms*
villain ['vɪlən] Verbrecher
debate Diskussion
valour ['vælə] Wagemut